whispers

whispers

poems from a thin place

charles r. ringma

AUREOLIN BLUE
Brisbane, Australia

Whispers
Copyright © 2025 Charles R. Ringma

Published by
Aureolin Blue
14 Greenway St.
Grange, Brisbane
Queensland 4051
Australia

All rights reserved. No part of this publication may be reproduced, stored in a retrieval system, or transmitted, in any form or by any means, electronic, mechanical, photocopying, recording or otherwise, without the prior written permission of the author, except in the case of brief quotations embodied in critical articles and reviews.

ISBN 978-1-57383-615-9

contents

preface / vii

the monks / 1
early morn / 3
dusk of day / 5
hope / 7
reborn / 9
to fall / 11
help for the helpless one? / 13
fingering the hem / 15
a safe place? / 17
a beautific smile / 19
receptivity and birthing / 21
conversion / 23
we are / 25
the mantra / 27
for eugene / 29
seeking / 31
clashing worlds / 33
surrender / 35
the elusive one / 37
the primal fall / 39
such contradictions / 41
the card player / 43
scattered / 45
having all / 47
trees / 49

the great silence / 51
a word / 53
the return / 55
god's apprentice? / 57
a tap on the window / 59
suffering / 61
love's gift / 63
for chip / 65
dementia / 67
a wounded man / 69
memories / 71
god's defence / 73
ode to kay / 75
o, my god! / 77
shedding / 79
an invitation to repentance / 81
drought / 83
a cry in the night / 85
the last dance / 87
whispers / 89
a troubled seeker / 91

notes / 93

preface

The night is not an enemy to be feared, but a friend who so often is neglected.

In the night, many sleep in deep repose. Others toss and turn like the waves of the sea. Some play. Others work. Others, clothed in the death-cloths of anxiety, wait for the morning.

And in the night monks pray longing for peace in a world of conflict.

Here lies the invitation.

So gently whispered.

So seldom heard.

In night's shadows there is presence.

In its stillness there are whispers.

In the night we may see so differently, devoid of the noise and clamour of our day.

Here the gentle spirit may brood over one's soul.

Here is a thin place.

Here a new world trembles to be reborn.

And from the womb of night, we may carry its light in the contours, and frequent madness, of our day. Whispers of the night may well become the songs of the day.

Charles Ringma
Brisbane, 2025

the monks

i join the monks
in the millennia
of longing,
sighing,
waiting,
praying,
singing,
serving.

in the ordinary rhythms
of *my* life
of working,
marriage,
children,
friends,
service,

i am carried
by *their* ancient tradition
of humility,
community,
hospitality,
conversion of life,
brotherhood,
faith.

i see them

these troubadours of the playful god
grounded,
joyful,
persevering,
faithful,
peaceful.

and i weep for my lack of courage
to walk with such fidelity –
me,
the comfortable inhabitant
of both worlds
wanting theirs and mine.
torn
between pristine faith and sheer pragmatism.

the monks
know this.
they see me.
and with eyes of compassionate faith
they hold me
in the midst of all my pain.

early morn

it's early sunday morn,
the world sleeps
and a mother weeps.

it's early sunday morn,
a cat strays
a monk prays.

it's
early sunday morn
rubbish bins are emptied
a lover is tempted.

it's early sunday morn
and no one hears
the raindrop of my tears.

dusk of day

in the late afternoon
which came too soon,
and the home rush
and the traffic crush,
with the worried mind
from the office grind,
she did not see
the ficus tree
bathed in the waning light
before sun's fall from sight.

and dusk's fingers
with the call to linger
was not seen or heard.

hope

we do all we can
that things will go well.
we plan.
we organise.
we implement.

and yet,
we hope for more.
some magic.
something beyond us.
like whispers of angels.
unseen.
unheard.
yet, present
in our aching hearts.

reborn

so,
do you just command –
you spectacle –
of sinai's fire and thunder.
and am I meant
in fear
and trembling
gladly to obey?

or,
do you lovingly persuade –
you victim –
of calvary's injustice.
and am i called
in gratitude
and faith
to grasp your sacrifice?

or,
do you silently awaken –
you guileless spirit –
of pentecost's outpouring.
and am i reborn
through water and blood
to be a new creation?

to fall

don't be afraid
to fall.

looking up
is better
than looking down.

from
places of security
we see
so little.

help for the helpless one?

i have often wondered
whether you need my help
you hidden and defenceless god?

a strange reversal this would be.
surely, i need *your* help
you god of power and grace.

and how would i aid you?
would our religious ceremonies suffice?
or do they hide your beauty?

could i offer hidden prayer?
a prophetic spirit?
a sacrificial love?
would that honour your name?

or, do you have to help yourself?
and do i wait
in dark corridors
for you
to fling open the heavy gates?

why, then, don't you rouse yourself –
you god of infinite patience.
disentangle yourself from joining
your sovereignty to our humanity!

be the wild one
in the extravagance of your love
and in the passion of your justice.
and like the hebrew slaves
of old
set us free.

fingering the hem

she could have touched
his hand,
his feet, perhaps.

but with gnarled
fingers
she fingered the hem of his garment
grimed on the palestinian road.

the softest of fabric
no longer pristine.
a picture perhaps
of her own wearied existence.

she had long thought
that this weariness had defined
her existence,
weighed down with illness and exclusion.

but she had heard his words,
seen his eyes,
and had fingered his heart.

the dusty hem
made her clean,
well,
whole.

a safe place?

is there a safe place
for us –
the satiated consumers,
the weary workers,
the worried parents,
the frustrated citizens?

is such a place
at a lover's breast,
in indulgent leisure,
in new beginnings,
in hesitant prayer?

or, are we condemned
to the longest longing,
the endless seeking,
the restless heart,
the never-ending journey?

is this safe place
a destination,
an inner disposition,
a fragile friendship,
a seeking faith?

can we hold it
with open hands?

can it nestle
in a broken heart?
can it descend
into fearful spaces?
can it well-up
in desert places?

a beautific smile

i caught
a mere glimpse
as she crossed the street
in her grey habit
and dangling prayer-beads.

but she looked
my way,
her smile was radiant
like the kiss of god.

what an intrusion
into such
a bleak day.

receptivity and birthing

all this talk
about male ways
being the primary mode
in your purposes, o god,
seems ever so odd,
so unlike you.

the word
has you birthing a world,
forming a people,
whom you nurture
like a child at a mother's breast.

theology
has you eternally
generating the son,
and ever at play
is your life-giving spirit.

and the life of faith
is not about
grasping and achieving,
but about reception
like a woman her lover.

and while men speak about
liberation,

and women about
mending,
st. francis – the odd one –
calls us to be a
birthing presence in your world.

receptivity
and
waiting,
birthing
and forming,
being
and doing.
a new world groaning into beauty.

conversion

we may need to be
converted
more
from our fanciful
certitudes,
than
from the folly
of our trivial
sins.

we are

we are the longest longing
an echo without end.
we are the greatest sighing
alone without a friend.
we are the greatest crying
o, lord, whom will you send?

we are the restless waiting
for much that is unseen.
we are the inward yearning
for what may yet have been.
we are a little dying
in the loss of every dream.

and yet we are the hoping
that springs eternal true.
we are the anxious praying
that has our eyes on you.
we the grateful receiving
that fills our hearts anew.

the mantra

in faith-communities
the mantra
is:
being found.

in daily life
the reality
is:
feeling lost.

in reflective spaces
the insight
is:
we seek again.

for eugene

he birthed
the word
in caverns
of the heart.
honed it
like a cello's haunting cry,
the swish of eagle's wings.

like an angel's breath,
like oil on aaron's beard,
the word
trembled,
groaned,
fructified.

but when he was
silent
bathed in attentiveness,
he also
spoke
of a way
beyond the edge of mystery.[1]

seeking

where are you
o mysterious and hidden one?
in my wildest imagination
for a better world?
in my yearnings
for happiness?
in the cry
from the depths of the human spirit?

am i meant to find you
in vaulting cathedrals?
in the melodies
of massed choirs?
in the pomp
of the universal church?
in liturgies, creeds, and theologies?

or, can no one really
find you?
does one wait to be
found?
do you come
like a flash of lighting in night's dark sky?
like a child
born before its expected time?

clashing worlds

the innocence of childhood
is long gone.
a naïve simplicity
has given way to inner conflicts.

though a protestant,
i bear the weight of a jewish grandmother.

though evangelical,
i long for the sacramental life.

though an australian,
i have a european heart.

though a westerner,
asia ever draws me.

though an urbanite,
the distant mountains ever call me.

though an academic,
social engagement ever prompts me.

though a father,
the monastery ever haunts me.

though a follower of jesus,
ordinary life ever attracts me.

though engaged with others,
being alone ever embraces me.

and though grateful for what i have,
i long for god's fulness of life.

surrender

and finally
the open hand,
so empty,
so vulnerable,
so cold,
so full of tears.

and now
the wait,
so fragile,
so uncertain,
yet so trusting,
so full of hope.

the elusive one

you have never appeared
with unambiguous clarity.

always a sudden appearing,
leaving us awed and wondering.

always the whisper of the spirit
and the flap of angel wings.

always the unsettling dream
and the irruption of an inner voice.

always a hint and a gentle nudge
and the task to grasp its meaning.

even the word lies mute
until you energise it.

and in the institutions we have made in your name,
you so seldom appear.

why so elusive, o god,
of creation and incarnation?

you want to be known,
and yet you are so hidden.

do you want us to make sense of this?
or do we just accept your strange ways?

do you have some purpose
in the unknowability of your mystery
and in the brightness of your revelation?

are you in fact, guarding yourself
from the way we may package you?

a wise move, i think,
if you don't mind me saying so.

best, that you continue to confound us.
otherwise, we will make you less than you are.

the primal fall

the first of our forebears
fell
free-fall
into the chaos of:
wrongful desire,
disobedience,
shame and blame.

everything was caught-up
in the slipstream
of this down-ward spiral:
a spurned god,
internal agitation,
a marred creation.

one would have thought
that everything should be done
to thrust us upward out of this fatal folly:
so full of despair
and disrepair.

but, no.
one has to fall again.
leaving self-effort
and the prowess of our ways,
to find

goodness
in the grace
of god's welcoming face.

such contradictions

found, yet o so lost;
at home, yet still wandering;
at peace, but disturbing thoughts still threaten;
in faith, but so uncertain;
in prayer, yet so many doubts;
in weariness, yet still sustained;
in doubt, but hope whispers;
alone, but thou art with me.

the card player

do you, o god,
keep the *kairos* moment
close to your chest,
like a card player
in some grimy backroom?

this moment is what we long for
in the march of dreary years,
when signs turn into the mirage
of a desert rain storm.

is waiting now our greatest calling,
rather than the wildness of dancing
in the upswing of your spirit
where the rivers flow?

your favourites,
simeon and anna,
grasped that moment with the baby boy
of *kairos* joy.

they waited long,
the years hung on them
like a worn-out cloak,
but their gaze was steady
and we, like them,
should now be ready.

scattered

he scattered
her ashes in the pond.
here, their children swam.
here, their friends had gathered.
here, they sat
in their latter years
watching the ducks,
and the setting sun
in the gentlest of a cooling breeze,
and the call of the currawong
heralding day's end.

the ashes
swam on the water's surface
with a vain attempt at survival.
he waited.
they sank into the pond's dark embrace.

but
she lies scattered elsewhere.
in the genetics
of children and grandchildren,
and in the gifts of hospitality,
in the memories
of those who have not forgotten
how much she loved and cared.

having all

having all,
seems
never enough.

having all,
may
have me in its grasp.

having all,
invites
the gift of generosity.

having all,
urges
the quest for a new freedom.

trees

those silent sentinels,
ever watchful,
ever dancing,
in the gentlest breeze.

deeply rooted,
they weave
a tapestry of connectedness,
holding fast what must not be lost.

their severed body
provides a home.
but their gaze on us is one of pity
as they no longer breathe for us.

the great silence

if i speak
out of the great silence
that invades
and purges me,
then little needs to be said.

but
its power
will be
a shaft of light,
that changes everything.

a word

long hoped for,
but unexpected
in that moment of time.

fragile,
melodious,
hidden in a donkey's stable.

embodied,
and some came to wonder,
but the powerful remained deaf to its music.

the return

an empty and dry land
sculpted by the fiercest of suns
and the blast of the desert moon,
home to a millennia of silence,
and the seldom movement of an ancient people,
and the folly of cattlemen
who ate dust instead of bread.

in this endless landscape
brown, flat, unyielding,
bereft of the sculpting hand of humanity,
a plume of dust
like an alter ego
shadows the moving spectre
of the solitary vehicle.

a young man in inner turmoil
goads his ute like a bucking steer
hoping that the welcome terrain of distance
will ease the pain,
and that the further horizon
will envelope and comfort him
like a woman's bellowing skirt.

but the lure of distance,
the hoped-for beyond,

and the embrace of the far-off arrival
is as dry as this bitter landscape.

wounds are not healed
in a desperate escape.
it is in returning
that reconciliation can become a two-step dance.

god's apprentice

o, mysterious one,
so seldom found and understood,
despite the cry of the prophets,
and the shame of golgotha's hill.

you hide more than you reveal,
and our chaotic world
shouts your absence,
reduces you to human fancy.

shall i come to your aid,
o, trinitarian lonely one,
banished from our world
and our hearts?

shall i cry with you in the fiercest storm?
glow with you in the embalming sun?
murmur with you in the cooing of doves?
joy with you in the birth of a child?
wing with you in the flight of your spirit?
join with you on the road of suffering?
weep with you in the lament of the ages?
dance with you when all is made well?

i wish, i could
shout your praises,
pray in desolation,

journey with your wayward people,
comfort a neighbour in distress,
mend a patch of your creation,
confront those who abuse their powers,
watch in the deepest darkness,
wait for the desert to bloom.

i wish.
the heart, is willing.
the resolve, o, so weak.

a tap on the window

surely, i can't see you, o hidden one.
the symbols of our worship
don't reflect the shadow of your face.

and
nature seems to breathe
its self-generated order and beauty.

and in my inner being
and in the face of others,
i only see a longing for what cannot be found.

so, can i hear you, o, silent one?
do you tap on my window,
like a twig in winter's storm?

or can i only touch you, o great untouchable,
in the embrace of lovers,
in the tokens of bread and wine?

but maybe, i just know you
in a long unknowing,
in a present absence,
in the air i breathe.

suffering

may our present
suffering –
which knocks on every door –
be a seed
that fructifies our pilgrimage.

but
in the mystery of faith –
which is ever a gift –
may this suffering
spawn a new world, waiting in birth-pains.

love's gift

love's
most gentlest gift –
a mother
singing a lullaby
to her new-born child.

love's
most common gift -
humanity's
care and gentleness
to friend and stranger.

love's
most seldom gift -
the seer
with the gift of ecstasy
in the flight of transcendence.

love's
brutal gift –
the lonely one
in sacrifice
for the greater good of others.

for chip

he had still planned
so many things –
even though the illness,
which had silently stalked him,
had shown its fatal intent.

a sculpture for his grandson,
a much-needed conversation with a friend,
family matters to process,
a family holiday,
heart issues long neglected.

and
who was to know
what was left unspoken.
thoughts buried in the darkest place.

but
the dark spectre
struck its fatal blow
in the midst of expectations.

he left life
unfinished.
so do we all.[2]

dementia

the partial sentence
hung in the room,
awkwardly,
like a skewed quarter moon
in a darkened sky.

everyone waited.
she tried again.
the words had faded.

she frowned.
hands flung into the air.
feet stamping.
and a whimpered whisper.

voices
filled the room again.
they washed over her
as she sank
beneath their waves.[3]

a wounded man

his literary
and academic successes
hung on him,
like a sodden army long-coat
in europe's appalling winter.

what could have been
a life-time's summer joy,
was
bitter ashes
for this wounded man.

his amazing abilities
came
not from a grateful heart,
but from the folly
of trying to appease
a father's stony silence.

memories

like scattered leaves
in the driest of summers,
so many memories
have faded,
disconnected from their life-giving source.

blown by the dry winds
of aging
and life's ever-changing circumstances,
they lie snared
among uprooted tree roots and barren boulders.

clothed in decay,
so brown, so brittle,
death gathers them.
but ever so unexpectedly,
green shoots appear,
the barren past bursts into life.

god's defence

what will you do
o, christian god
in your own defence?
does your rejection by so many
pain you?

are you expecting
the church
to come to your aid,
she, who is often clothed with shame,
and her undergarments
are the colour of indifference?

surely,
you will need
to rouse yourself,
though
unruly power and vengeance,
are not your way.

maybe
you are already
fully in the fray,
leaving us to our follies,
till pain and longing
and the promptings of your spirit
make us cry out to you?

ode to kay

it was
in a moment of time
like
a soft sigh
that she slipped away.

maybe
long ago
she
had already journeyed
with
the eyes of faith
to
that other world?

she
the sparkling one,
of
generous heart,
of
splendid curiosity,
of
gracious hospitality.

she
lingers
embodied in family

and
in the grateful hearts
of
all who were brushed
by
her gracious spirit.

and
her prayers
of
this mortal life
still
hover over all
for
whom she had compassion.[4]

o, my god!

how is it
that you have become
such a problem?

they say,
that you sow self-righteousness
and cause bigotry and wars.

it is just, is it not,
that you should be removed
from public life?

as your tenuous lover
i have to agree.
but we have made you thus.

we
sought to make you
our own
and killed you.

we
are your betrayers,
not
the secular world.

shedding

the hallelujah chorus
of the kookaburras
woke me.

it was 3am
with the sound of
crashing,

and
the bush-curlew's
warning cry.

more crashes,
unfamiliar,
threatening.

uncertain,
but i drift
to a troubled sleep.

morning light,
and a deck
full of far-flung strips of bark.

the shedding
grey gum,
now naked in the gleaming sun.

so much
crashing,
yet new life.

invitation to repentance

i wait
in fearful expectation
in the longest
silence
for a word
that should be flung into the world's
madness.

but
when it comes
with
brooding presence
and
scathing light,

it
exposes me
long
before it is cast
into the world's
sadness.

drought

a brazen blue,
unforgiving as the night,
a closed womb,
no rain in sight.

the brown earth cries,
a lament of the ages,
everything dies,
a requiem in its pages.

and in the long wait,
for the heavens to weep,
farmers gave up,
despair went too deep.

land and beast whimper,
cursed is the ground,
no prayer is offered,
no priest is found.

a cry in the night

i awake
startled and afraid.
what
was i dreaming?
what
was lost in not remembering?

then,
i hear it again
the eerie call of the bush curlew,
triggering my tears
for –
a wounded humanity,
an exploited earth,
a crisis in leadership,
the loss of civility,
and
the folly of my own life.

the curlew
cries again,
but
i am already
falling
into a troubled sleep.

the last dance

she
heaved a sigh,
her
world up-ended.

a
life of shadows
all
pretended.

and
spiralling down
with
furrowed frown
the pain
was lanced.

and
for the first time
she
danced.

whispers

he almost held
the whisper
in his
tender-fingered hand.

like grasping
the scent
of the silver wattle
in a moment of
ecstasy.

he splayed the whisper
on canvass,
as markers in sand dunes,
as insights in a lecture hall,
like
a profligate spender.

the whisper
ever held him
in the membranes of his
heart,
and its beauty
pregnant,
a healing to
impart.[5]

a troubled seeker

there is nothing
winsome
about you,
o, difficult one.

you are playful in your
wildness,
severe in your
mercy,
tempestuous in your
silence,
bounded in your
power,
silent in your
speaking,
frightening in your
spirit.

and yet
i draw closer
with tiptoe curiosity,
sculpted
out of an ancient memory,
of having known
you
before the world

became your brutal
burden.[6]

notes

1. Dr. Eugene Peterson, author of *The Message* and colleague at Regent College, Vancouver, passed away in 2018.
2. Chip Hedges, a long-time friend, passed away in 2021.
3. In memory of our friend, Angie Andrews, who suffers from the early onset of dementia.
4. Kay Brothers passed away in 2023—a dear friend who radiated the fragrance of Christ with wild abandon.
5. In memory of Dr. Lindsay Farrell, artist, academic, carer for humanity. He passed away in 2020.
6. Charles Ringma, *Ragged Edges: Poems from the Margins* (Aureolin Blue, 2008), 13.

contact:

www.charlesringma.com
holyscribblers.blogspot.com